Serenity Now!!

Serenity Now!!

HOW TO GET HAPPY IN A HURRY

—

Bradley W. Rasch

ISBN: 1981669507
ISBN 13: 9781981669509

Introduction

———

EVERYONE WANTS TO BE HAPPY. Everyone wants serenity now!

It is something we all pursue, and a state of mind we want for our loved ones and ourselves. This book will give you the tools to achieve happiness and serenity. It will help you get your mind right, the first step on the journey to serenity now. We do have control over our beliefs, values, and goals. These come first, and then come our actions.

Let us first define some terms, so we are all on the same page:

1. Happiness "a state of well-being and contentment"
2. Serenity: "The state of being calm, peaceful, and untroubled."

Lets get started.

Contents

CHAPTER 1

Keep Your Friends Close

—

**"Friendship consists in forgetting what one gives
and remembering what one receives".**

— ALEXANDER DUMAS

MOST OF US CAN COUNT our real friends on one hand and still have a few fingers left over. That's okay; the good things in life are not always in abundance, all the more reason to cherish them.

Our good friends, our true friends, provide us with a number of important things, not the least of which is really good memories, something no one can take from us. People tend to reciprocate; it is a strong motivator of human behavior. If you want someone to be your friend, give them your friendship, they are likely to return the favor.

There is no statute of limitations on adding friends to your "posse". You can do it at anytime of life.

People with close friends tend to be happier and healthier emotionally and physically. Friends are the family we choose.

Like anything else important and valuable, it is something we have to work at. Just as it is important to invest in your education and your home, it is important to invest in your friendships. Work at them, invest in them, and they will pay dividends, for you and for those that choose to be your friend.

"The greatest gift of life is friendship, and I have received it".

— HUBERT H. HUMPHREY

CHAPTER 2

Quit Your Complaining

—

"Never tell your problems to anyone...20% don't care
and the other 80% are glad you have them."

— LOU HOLTZ

IF YOU ARE COMPLAINING, USUALLY you are not looking for solutions.

Social Scientists will tell you that no one wants to be around a complainer. We prefer to be around people that are positive, that lift our mood. Be one of those people.

Not only do people not want to be around a complainer, many folks actively avoid them, and generally do not see them as friendship material. We of course are talking about chronic complainers here.

Rather than spending energy complaining, put that energy into solving the problem. If you seek people to help you solve a problem, more often than not, they will be receptive to helping. If you complain, and complain, they may tune you out, and perceive you as a whiner, and not a problem solver.

"The tendency to whining and complaining may be taken as the
surest sign symptom of little souls and inferior intellects".

— FRANCIS JEFFREY

CHAPTER 3

Clear The Air Politely

—

"You shall know the truth, and the truth shall make you mad."

Not addressing issues almost always makes a situation worse. They do not get better over time (exception-fine wine stored properly).

Addressing problems you can fix leads to being a happier person than ignoring them and letting them fester.

If the problem involves another person, address it politely, not in terms of assigning blame, but as a request for help in dealing with a problem.

"People learn to treat you based on what you accept from them".

CHAPTER 4

Find Your Inner Beauty

—

"Beauty is when you can appreciate yourself. When you
love yourself, that's when you're most beautiful".

— Zoe Kravitz

WE ALL HAVE AN INNER beauty. Sometimes we do not realize it, and sometimes we are aware of it, and are not thankful for it, or do not appreciate it. Celebrate it modestly. If you do not, no one else will.

"Life is full of beauty. Notice it. Notice the bumblebee, the small
child, and the smiling faces. Smell the rain, and feel the wind. Live
your life to the fullest potential, and fight for your dreams".

— Ashley Smith

CHAPTER 5

Give It Your Best Shot

———

"Always Do Your Best. Your best is going to change from
moment to moment; it will be different when you are healthy as
opposed to sick. Under any circumstance, simply do your best,
and you will avoid self-judgment, self-abuse and regret"

— DON MIGUEL RUIZ

ALL OF US WANT TO reach our maximum potential. That is human nature. All of us are somewhat unhappy if we do not. Especially if we do not even try. Reaching our potential in our relationships with others, our work, our hobbies, and our spiritual lives is important to our emotional well-being. We can accept not reaching our absolute potential, if we have made the effort, given it our best shot.

James Allen once said: "All that you achieve and all that you fail to achieve is the direct result of your thoughts".

So let's get our minds right.

"I believe that in life, you have to give things your best
shot, do your best. You have to focus on what needs to be
done, do the right thing, not the popular thing".

— DAVID CAMERON

CHAPTER 6

Bury The Past

———

"Yesterday is gone. Tomorrow has not yet come.
We have only today. Let us begin."

— Mother Theresa

We can't change the past, so why do we spend so much time ruminating about it? Why torture yourself? Make use of the experience, and use it as a positive. Be in the present.

"The present changes the past. Looking back
you do not find what you left behind."

— Kiran Desai

CHAPTER 7

Take A Big Picture Perspective

———

"To be a champion, I think you have to see the big picture. It's
not about winning and losing; it's about every day hard work and
about thriving on a challenge. It's about embracing the pain that
you'll experience at the end of a race and not being afraid. I think
people think too hard and get afraid of a certain challenge."

— SUMMER SANDERS

ALWAYS LOOK AT HE BIG Picture. What are your long-term goals? What is
important to you? Things will come up day-to-day that are frustrating. Do
not let them frustrate you; keep your eye on your goals, the Big Picture. Don't
let them distract you.

"In order to properly understand the big picture,
everyone should fear becoming mentally clouded and
obsessed with one small section of truth."

— XUN KUANG

CHAPTER 8

Value Your Friends

———

"Friends show their love in times of trouble, not in happiness."

— Euripides

Value your friends. They are important. Friends are the family we choose. Want to make a friend? Give someone your friendship. Friendship gives you much joy, especially when you are the giver. Psychologists will tell you that it is the giver that is the happiest. As we get older, true friends become more important to us. Having close friends not only makes us happier, but healthier.

"Walking with a friend in the dark is better
than walking alone in the light."

— Helen Keller

CHAPTER 9

Practice Tolerance

———

"Hatred is corrosive of a person's wisdom and conscience; the
mentality of enmity can poison a nation's spirit, instigate brutal
life and death struggles, destroy a society's tolerance and humanity,
and block a nation's progress to freedom and democracy."

— Liu Xiaobo

The Golden Rule is certainly a good rule to live by. Do unto others…. Others often treat us as we treat them. If we are tolerant of others, more than likely others will be tolerant of us. It is important for us to not only talk the talk, but also walk our talk. If we believe in tolerance, and espouse it, we should live it.

"Tolerance, compromise, understanding, acceptance, patience
- I want those all to be very sharp tools in my shed".

— CeeLo Green

CHAPTER 10

Push The Envelope

—

"See your life as a giant adventure. Keep pushing the envelope,
and remember that every dream starts off small."

— Robin Sharma

OFTEN WE SET LIMITS FOR ourselves. Sometimes because our elders suggest it, at other times we do so because culture encourages us to. We are never more alive than when we push the limits, push the envelope. As long as you are not hurting anyone, or thinking solely of yourself, move to the edge and live.

"I like pushing the envelope. But I don't like
to do it just for the sake of doing it."

— Madonna

CHAPTER 11

Keep The Faith

—

"Optimism is the faith that leads to achievement. Nothing
can be done without hope and confidence".

— HELEN KELLER

FAITH MAKES US STRONGER AND more resilient. Things are never as bad as they seem (unless you were a Cubs fan before 2016). Optimistic folks are happier, more productive, healthier, and more content. They tend to achieve more. Just as importantly, people enjoy being around them. People that are extremely pessimistic are often avoided. Optimism and pessimism tend to be somewhat contagious.

"Keep your dreams alive. Understand to achieve anything requires
faith and belief in yourself, vision, hard work, determination, and
dedication. Remember all things are possible for those who believe."

— GAIL DEVERS

CHAPTER 12

Explore The Unknown

——

"We can't be afraid of change. You may feel very secure in the
pond that you are in, but if you never venture out of it, you
will never know that there is such a thing as an ocean, a sea.
Holding onto something that is good for you now, may be
the very reason why you don't have something better."

— **C. JOY BELL C**

THE WORLD IS CHANGING AT a furious pace. More so than at any other time
in human history. Do not fear change embrace it. Keep up with it. If you
do, you will maintain an energy and curiosity that will serve you well. Enjoy
change. Enjoy learning new things. It keeps you young and engaged. Ask
questions. People love answering them. We learn more by listening than
talking.

"As for me, I am tormented with an everlasting itch for things
remote. I love to sail forbidden seas, and land on barbarous coasts."

— **HERMAN MELVILLE**

Love and Work

—

"Your work is going to fill a large part of your life, and the only
way to be truly satisfied is to do what you believe is great work.
And the only way to do great work is to love what you do."

— STEVE JOBS

SIGMUND FREUD SAID A WHOLE lot of things that are not taken very seriously by psychologists in current times. Don't even get me started about that whole penis envy thing. Nonetheless, he did make some solid contributions in terms of understanding human behavior, and our subject at hand: happiness. Freud postulated that to be truly fulfilled, truly happy, one must find a high level of purpose in work and love. To reach a high level of contentment, a person needs to feel they have made a difference, a contribution in their chosen work, whatever it may be. A person must also have loved, contributed to another they care about.

Okay Sigmund, sometimes a cigar is just a cigar…. just sayin.

"There is only one happiness in this life, to love and be loved."

— GEORGE SAND

CHAPTER 14

Keep Milhausing

—

"Take care of your body. It's the only place you have to live."

— Jim Rohn

Every time I see my physician he tells me to "keep Milhausing." Is he a real Doctor? Yes. And a very good one.

Not long ago I was quite unhealthy. My physician insisted I hire a personal trainer that really knew what he or she was doing. That led me to Milhaus. MIlhaus runs a gym in Carol Stream, Illinois (a Chicago suburb) called TRIM. This trainer got me to the point where I exercise vigorously at least one hour a day. He pointed out that a positive life style change would occur if I felt quite lousy on a day I did *not* workout.

Milhaus was able to help me achieve a fitness level that allowed me to ditch seven medications and become a whole lot healthier. A serious everyday exercise program also allowed me to be happier. As a psychologist I knew this was important, and I finally experienced it.

How does serious exercise make you happier? Certainly, you feel accomplished that you have exercised everyday. You feel better about yourself, especially as compared to your more sedentary peers. But wait, there is more. There is actually a chemical component.

Ever hear of the "runners high." It is real. When someone exercises vigorously their body produces endorphins. Endorphins make you feel content, you feel a heightened sense of wellness, of happiness. In fact, for very mild depression, the blues if you will, many psychologists recommend regular exercise. Exercise is just as effective, or more effective, in many cases, for the improvement of mood than pharmacological intervention, or talk therapy.

Very current research strongly suggests that regular exercise not only impacts mood in a positive way, but also puts you at less risk for losses in cognitive functioning and memory loss.

So keep Milhausing!!

"Reading is to the mind what exercise is to the body."

— Joseph Addison

CHAPTER 15

Chris Cross, Sailing, and the Canvass

—

"Today is life-the only life you are sure of. Make the most
of today. Get interested in something. Shake yourself
awake. Develop a hobby. Let the winds of enthusiasm
sweep through you. Live today with gusto."

— DALE CARNEGIE

IN 1979 RECORDING ARTIST CHRISTOPHER Cross penned the tune "Sailing". It was not really a tune about sailing; it was a statement about the importance of hobbies and pursuing interests that you enjoy. Here is a small snippet of the lyrics:

"Well, it's not far down to paradise, at least it's not for me
And if the wind is right you can sail away and find tranquility
Oh, the canvas can do miracles, just you wait and see
Believe me"

Hobbies are important to happiness. It is important to have and to pursue your interests. Even FDR who presided over the Great Depression and the Second World War found time to work on and enjoy his stamp collection. Having a hobby or hobbies, something you love to do, is an important component towards fulfillment. Find one and pursue it with passion.

When working as a Child Psychologist, I often recommended to parents of very ill children to encourage their child to find and engage with an enjoyable hobby. Doing so not only lessened the child's stress, it allowed them to focus on something they loved, and they were, to a child, much happier.

Enhance your life. Find a hobby. Enjoy it.

"Everything I do is part of my passion. I do the things I like to do. It's sort of a bigger version of having more than one hobby. I love to play piano, sing, and act. I love to do all those things."

— Harry Connick, Jr.

Smart Phones and Social Media in Moderation

—

"The more time we spend interconnected via a myriad of devices, the less time we have left to develop true friendships in the real world."

— ALEX MORRITT

MANY OF US ARE SPENDING a lot of time on social media, and a tremendous amount of time on our smart phones. A high percentage of smart phone owners will touch their phones 2,617 times a day. An average thirteen -year old smart phone Social media user will check social media up to 100 times a day. Smart phone addiction is a real issue. When a person checks their smart phone and finds a "like" or a text from someone their brain secretes dopamine, the same chemical that occurs when some addictive recreational drugs are consumed. So for some, checking the smart phone, checking social media, can be addicting.

Some of the greatest experiences in life are experienced through our smart phones. People that have the once in a lifetime opportunity to see a significant person: the Pope, a President, a Movie Star, etc, do so through the lens of their smart phone. Why? Why not enjoy that moment in reality, and not through your phone. Trust me, you can obtain a lot of pictures of that person that will be better than the one you took from your smart phone. The rare moment you experienced will always be remembered even if you did not take a picture of the person with your smart phone. Without the phone use, maybe you could even have interacted with this individual. A real human interaction.

Often when we are actually with friends or loved ones in person, we are still interacting with distant people via our phones, and giving little attention to the people that are physically before us. What does that tell them about our feelings for them? What does it tell us about us?

Recent research suggests that heavy social media users are more at risk for depression in many cases. They compare themselves to the glamorous posts of their friends, and feel inadequate.

Consider limiting your smart phone usage and social media usage. Invest more time in the real world there before you. You will be happier for it.

> "What social-media really becomes after years of use is a
> constant stream of information both verbal and visual that at
> first drenches the mind, quenching its thirst for knowledge,
> and subduing its curiosity slowly but surly transforms into a
> torrent that renders the brain heavy and the mind restless."
>
> — Aysha Taryam

CHAPTER 17

All You Need is Love: Spread it Around

—

"Love is when the other person's happiness is
more important than your own."

— H. Jackson Brown, Jr.

The Captain and Tenille were right: Love Will Keep Us Together. Love binds us to others specifically and generally. It validates our lives, gives it meaning. It allows us to care about others. You cannot give to someone else what you do not have. So love yourself so you can love others. Spread it around. You will make someone else happier. You will make yourself happier.

"Love is friendship that has caught fire. It is quiet
understanding, mutual confidence, sharing and forgiving. It
is loyalty through good and bad times. It settles for less than
perfection and makes allowances for human weaknesses."

— Ann Landers

CHAPTER 18

Focus

"Live life to the fullest, and focus on the positive."

— MATT CAMERON

GET FOCUSED. DECIDE WHAT YOU want to accomplish, and focus on that. Do not let the small things bother you. Having goals helps us focus on what is important to us, and allows us to not "sweat the small stuff."

If we do not have goals, things we want to accomplish, we wander aimlessly through life, not a pleasant feeling. Goals can involve improving our relationships, helping others, getting in shape, having a great garden, learning a second language, the list goes on…

"Successful people maintain a positive focus in life no matter what
is going on around them. They stay focused on their past successes
rather than their past failures, and on the next action steps they
need to take to get them closer to the fulfillment of their goals
rather than all the other distractions that life presents to them."

— JACK CANFIELD

CHAPTER 19

Slow Down You Move Too Fast

—

"Slow down, you move too fast
You got to make the morning last
Just kicking down the cobblestones
Looking for fun and feelin' groovy
Ba da da da da da da, feelin' groovy"

— Paul Simon

I sincerely hope you do not hear this song in your head all day. It is a great song, but still…

Sometimes we have to slow down a bit and enjoy life. Certainly not when the light turns green during rush hour and there is a long line of motorists behind us (I speak from experience).

Most of our life involves rushing. Rushing through meetings at work, rushing to service a client, to do housework so we can enjoy a little down time. You have been there, you know what I mean.

Inevitably, our leisure time comes. It is well deserved. We want to make the most of it. This is right and proper. But sometimes, we rush through it. We plan on taking a walk in the woods, catch lunch, and then catch a movie on our day off. Let's do that woods in a half hour, we have much to do. No!! Enjoy the woods. Slow walk it. Appreciate what is before you. You have done enough rushing this week. They will cook for you when you arrive, and there is more than one movie start time. And if you only complete your nature walk, if you have taken the time to enjoy it, it is all for the better.

"Slow down and enjoy life. It's not only the scenery you miss by going
to fast - you also miss the sense of where you are going and why."

— Eddie Cantor

CHAPTER 20

But Don't Waste It

———

"Thirty years ago my older brother, who was ten years old at the time, was trying to get a report written on birds that he'd had three months to write, which was due the next day. We were out at our family cabin in Bolinas, and he was at the kitchen table close to tears, surrounded by binder paper and pencils and unopened books about birds, immobilized by the hugeness of the task ahead. Then my father sat down beside him put his arm around my brother's shoulder, and said, "Bird by bird, buddy. Just take it bird by bird.""

— **ANNE LAMOTT, BIRD BY BIRD: SOME INSTRUCTIONS ON WRITING AND LIFE**

OH BOY, I JUST TOLD you to slow down, please do, on occasion. You deserve it, and it is necessary. It must be pointed out however, that time is our most precious commodity. We all are given a finite amount of it. Do not waste it. The fact that our time is finite is a blessing. It encourages us to set goals, and to value our time, to use it well. Set your priorities and make sure your time is spent there first- your family and loved ones. Apportion some to y0ur career, to your enjoyable past times. Plan well and y0u will not waste.

"Time is the most valuable coin in your life. You and you alone will determine how that coin will be spent. Be careful that you do not let other people spend it for you."

— **CARL SANDBURG**

CHAPTER 21

Get In Touch With Your Creative Side

—

"Art, freedom and creativity will change society faster than politics."

— Victor Pinchuk

Socrates said: "Wisdom begins in wonder." Not bad advice. Wonder. All of us have very strong creative powers. Ideas to offer, solutions to propose. Unleash your creativity. Don't be ashamed of it. It is a powerful force. Use your creativity in your hobbies, employ it at work. You will be more fulfilled,

"Creativity is putting your imagination to work, and it's
produced the most extraordinary results in human culture."

— Ken Robinson

CHAPTER 22

Get Ready

—

"Opportunity doesn't make appointments, you
have to be ready when it arrives."

— TIM FARGO

IF YOU WANT TO WIN a marathon you have to be ready. You must train for hours religiously. If you want to get into medical school, you have to study and work hard for a long period of time. You have to be ready. You have to put in the work. Want that part in a movie? You have to have the experience, make contacts, and go to hundreds of auditions. You have to be ready. In short, to get ready means to pay your dues.

"I never met a girl who makes me feel the way that you do
(It's alright)
Whenever I'm asked who makes my dreams real
I say that you do
(you're outta sight)
So fee fi fo fum
Look out baby 'cause here I come
And I'm bringing you a love that's true so get ready
So get ready
So get ready here I come
I'm on my way"

— THE TEMPTATIONS

You Are Not Your Job

—

"You are not your job, you're not how much money you
have in the bank. You are not the car you drive. You're
not the contents of your wallet. You are not your khakis.
You are all singing, all dancing of the world."

— Chuck Palahniuk, Fight Club

You are not your career. A job, a job well done, is important to a sense of contentment. However, you are not your career. You are first a child, parent, sibling, aunt, uncle, cousin, mentor, or friend. If you change jobs, do so with a positive outlook. That will go a long way towards fulfillment.

"The Gift of Balance in Your Life - May you find the balance
of life, time for work but also time for play. Too much of one
thing ends up creating stress that no one needs in their life."

— Catherine Pulsifer

All We Are Saying Is Give Peace A Chance

"Do not let the behavior of others destroy your inner peace."

— Dalai Lama

No person no thing has the ability to keep you from finding peace, unless you allow them or the circumstances to. If something is standing in the way of attaining peace, act to remove it. If it is something you cannot change, do not worry about it. Worrying about things we cannot change accomplishes nothing. Achieving peace is something you can do, if you decide to do it.

"If there's no inner peace, people can't give it to you.
The husband can't give it to you. Your children can't
give it to you. You have to give it to you."

— Linda Evans

Update Your Goals

—

"The New Year stands before us, like a chapter in a book, waiting
to be written. We can help write that story by setting goals."

— MELODY BEATTIE

ALL ACCOMPLISHED PEOPLE SET GOALS. The most successful athletes always pursue a personal best. Without goals we do not know where we are going-an unpleasant state of affairs. Reset your goals periodically. Give yourself a positive direction.

"I don't focus on what I'm up against. I focus on
my goals and I try to ignore the rest."

— VENUS WILLIAMS

Discover Your Passion

—

"Far and away the best prize that life offers is the
chance to work hard at work worth doing."

— THEODORE ROOSEVELT

FIND OUT WHAT YOUR PASSION is and pursue it. It could be your job, volunteering to help others, swimming, or baking the Best chocolate chip cookie
this world has ever known.

You won't find your passion unless you search for it. Embrace it when you
find it. It's yours. Everyone deserves one (or more)!

"Build your own dreams, or someone else will hire you to build theirs."

— FARRAH GRAY

Face Your Fears

—

"You gain strength, courage, and confidence by every
experience in which you really stop to look fear in the
face. You are able to say to yourself, 'I lived through this
horror. I can take the next thing that comes along."

— ELEANOR ROOSEVELT

FACE YOUR FEARS. THEY WILL own you until you do. Easy for me to say, but trust me, you will be glad you did. The more you do it, the better you can do it. Before you know it, you will be fearless. Nothing wrong with asking for a little help or guidance along the way. As your fears diminish you will grow.

"Remember your dreams and fight for them. You must know
what you want from life. There is just one thing that makes
your dream become impossible: the fear of failure."

— PAULO COELHO

CHAPTER 28

Sometimes You Have To Ask For Directions

—

"The most important thing I think we need to remember is
that we're a work in progress. Do not be ashamed or afraid
to ask for help. That's what I did. I asked for help."

— CARNIE WILSON

OKAY GUYS LISTEN UP. SOMETIMES you have to ask for direction; sometimes you have to ask for a little help. How do *you* feel when someone asks you for help? Honored. So honor someone you respect when you need direction. They will be glad you asked. No one does it alone. We all stand on the shoulders of others. A humble and confident person is not afraid to ask for a little help every now and again.

"Nothing can stop the man with the right mental
attitude from achieving his goal; nothing on earth can
help the man with the wrong mental attitude."

— THOMAS JEFFERSON

CHAPTER 29

Be A Trailblazer

—

"The hope of a secure and livable world lies with disciplined
nonconformists, who are dedicated to justice, peace and brotherhood.
The trailblazers in human, academic, scientific and religious freedom
have always been nonconformists. In any cause that concerns the
progress of mankind, put your faith in the nonconformist!"

— MARTIN LUTHER KING, JR.

TRY BEING A TRAILBLAZER. READ a different newspaper than usual in the
morning, have something new for breakfast, try a different route to work. On
the job, apply a different approach to a task. Build on this. Become someone
different. Learn to innovate. Get in the habit of making changes, one step at
a time, set the goal of becoming an innovator, a trailblazer.

"The trailblazers are my role models in this industry:
Sidney Poitier, Harry Belafonte, James Earl Jones, and
Billy Dee Williams. I keep their pictures in my trailer and
try to measure to their standards every time I act."

— BRIAN J. WHITE

CHAPTER 30

Set Priorities

———

"Action expresses priorities."

— MAHATMA GANDHI

EVERY DAY YOU HAVE A huge to do list. Know what your priorities are before you tackle it.

When the author worked as a Child Psychologist, when parents asked for help, they were always asked to fill out ten index cards with their most important priorities on them. They were asked to write one goal on each card, one thing important to them. If something that related to their child did not appear on a single card, they were asked to come back when their child or their child's needs could find a way onto one of the cards.

"Our life is the sum total of all the decisions we make every
day, and those decisions are determined by Our priorities."

— MYLES MUNROE

Listen to Leo

—

"Your talent is God's gift to you. What you do
with it is your gift back to God."

— LEO BUSCAGLIA

"Too often we underestimate the power of a touch, a smile, a kind
word, a listening ear, an honest compliment, or the smallest act of
caring, all of which have the potential to turn a life around."

— LEO BUSCAGLIA

"Worry never robs tomorrow of its sorrow, it only saps today of its joy."

— LEO BUSCAGLIA

"A single rose can be my garden... a single friend, My world."

— LEO BUSCAGLIA

"I still get wildly enthusiastic about little things... I play with
leaves. I skip down the street and run against the wind."

— LEO BUSCAGLIA

"I believe that you control your destiny, that you can be what you want
to be. You can also stop and say, 'No, I won't do it; I won't behave
his way anymore. I'm lonely and I need people around me, maybe
I have to change my methods of behaving,' and then you do it."

— LEO BUSCAGLIA

"We want to gently remind people that we don't have forever. In my work, I hear parents complain all the time that their children grow up so fast. But they don't take the time to sit down and talk to each other. The last bastion of getting together is around the table."

— Leo Buscaglia

"Love is always open arms. If you close your arms about love you will find that you are left holding only yourself."

— Leo Buscaglia

CHAPTER 32

Know What Stage Of Life You And Others Are in

———

ERICK ERICKSON WAS A GIFTED psychologist that developed the theory we will discuss below. Erickson's theory suggests that we are social by nature, and that we all go through stages in our lives. We have an important struggle at each stage. We can negotiate this stage in a positive or negative way. Each stage holds something that is important to us. Each stage allows us to develop a virtue. If we understand what stage someone is in, we understand them, and their priorities better. We also understand their struggles. We know ourselves better if we understand these stages of life.

1. TRUST VS. MISTRUST

Is the world a safe place or is it full of unpredictable events and accidents waiting to happen? Erikson's first psychosocial crisis occurs during the first year or so of life (like Freud's oral stage of psychosexual development). The crisis is one of trust vs. mistrust.

During this stage, the infant is uncertain about the world in which they live. To resolve these feelings of uncertainty, the infant looks towards their primary caregiver for stability and consistency of care.

If the care the infant receives is consistent, predictable and reliable, they will develop a sense of trust, which will carry with them to other relationships, and they will be able to feel secure even when threatened.

Success in this stage will lead to the virtue of **hope**. By developing a sense of trust, the infant can have hope that as new crises arise, there is a real possibility that other people will be there as a source of support. Failing to acquire the virtue of hope will lead to the development of fear.

For example, if the care has been harsh or inconsistent, unpredictable and unreliable, then the infant will develop a sense of mistrust and will not have confidence in the world around them or in their abilities to influence events.

This infant will carry the basic sense of mistrust with them to other relationships. It may result in anxiety, heightened insecurities, and an over feeling of mistrust in the world around them.

Consistent with Erikson's views on the importance of trust, research by Bowlby and Ainsworth has outlined how the quality of the early experience of attachment can affect relationships with others in later life.

2. Autonomy vs. Shame and Doubt

The child is developing physically and becoming more mobile. Between the ages of 18 months and three, children begin to assert their independence, by walking away from their mother, picking which toy to play with, and making choices about what they like to wear, to eat, etc.

The child is discovering that he or she has many skills and abilities, such as putting on clothes and shoes, playing with toys, etc. Such skills illustrate the child's growing sense of independence and autonomy. Erikson states it is critical that parents allow their children to explore the limits of their abilities within an encouraging environment, which is tolerant of failure.

For example, rather than put on a child's clothes a supportive parent should have the patience to allow the child to try until they succeed or ask for assistance. So, the parents need to encourage the child to become more independent while at the same time protecting the child so that constant failure is avoided.

A delicate balance is required from the parent. They must try not to do everything for the child, but if the child fails at a particular task they must not criticize the child for failures and accidents (particularly when toilet training). The aim has to be "self control without a loss of self-esteem". Success in this stage will lead to the virtue of **will**.

If children in this stage are encouraged and supported in their increased independence, they become more confident and secure in their own ability to survive in the world.

If children are criticized, overly controlled, or not given the opportunity to assert themselves, they begin to feel inadequate in their ability to survive, and may then become overly dependent upon others, lack self-esteem, and feel a sense of shame or doubt in their abilities.

3. Initiative vs. Guilt

Around age three and continuing to age five, children assert themselves more frequently. These are particularly lively, rapid-developing years in a child's life. According to Bee it is a "time of vigor of action and of behaviors that the parents may see as aggressive."

During this period the primary feature involves the child regularly interacting with other children at school. Central to this stage is play, as it provides children with the opportunity to explore their interpersonal skills through initiating activities.

Children begin to plan activities, make up games, and initiate activities with others. If given this opportunity, children develop a sense of initiative and feel secure in their ability to lead others and make decisions.

Conversely, if this tendency is squelched, either through criticism or control, children develop a sense of guilt. They may feel like a nuisance to others and will, therefore, remain followers, lacking in self-initiative.

The child takes initiatives, which the parents will often try to stop in order to protect the child. The child will often overstep the mark in his forcefulness, and the danger is that the parents will tend to punish the child and restrict his initiatives too much.

It is at this stage that the child will begin to ask many questions as his thirst for knowledge grows. If the parents treat the child's questions as trivial, a nuisance or embarrassing or other aspects of their behavior as threatening then the child may have feelings of guilt for "being a nuisance".

Too much guilt can make the child slow to interact with others and may inhibit their creativity. Some guilt is, of course, necessary; otherwise the child would not know how to exercise self-control or have a conscience.

A healthy balance between initiative and guilt is important. Success in this stage will lead to the virtue of **purpose**.

4. Industry (competence) vs. Inferiority

Industry versus inferiority is the fourth stage of Erik Erikson's theory of psychosocial development. The stage occurs during childhood between the ages of five and twelve.

Children are at the stage where they will be learning to read and write, to do sums, to do things on their own. Teachers begin to take an important role in the child's life as they teach the child specific skills.

It is at this stage that the child's peer group will gain greater significance and will become a major source of the child's self-esteem. The child now feels the need to win approval by demonstrating specific competencies that are valued by society and begin to develop a sense of pride in their accomplishments.

If children are encouraged and reinforced for their initiative, they begin to feel industrious and feel confident in their ability to achieve goals. If this initiative is not encouraged, if it is restricted by parents or teacher, then the child begins to feel inferior, doubting his own abilities and therefore may not reach his or her potential.

If the child cannot develop the specific skill they feel society is demanding (e.g., being athletic) then they may develop a sense of inferiority. Some failure may be necessary so that the child can develop some modesty. Again, a balance between competence and modesty is necessary. Success in this stage will lead to the virtue of **competence**.

5. IDENTITY VS. ROLE CONFUSION

The fifth stage is identity vs. role confusion, and it occurs during adolescence, from about 12-18 years. During this stage, adolescents search for a sense of self and personal identity, through an intense exploration of personal values, beliefs, and goals.

The adolescent mind is essentially a mind or moratorium, a psychosocial stage between childhood and adulthood, and between the morality learned by the child, and the ethics to be developed by the adult during adolescence, the transition from childhood to adulthood is most important. Children are becoming more independent, and begin to look at the future in terms of career, relationships, families, housing, etc. The individual wants to belong to a society and fit in.

This is a major stage of development where the child has to learn the <u>roles</u> he will occupy as an adult. It is during this stage that the adolescent will re-examine his identity and try to find out exactly who he or she is. Erikson suggests that two identities are involved: the sexual and the occupational.

According to Bee, what should happen at the end of this stage is "a reintegrated sense of self, of what one wants to do or be, and of one's appropriate sex role". During this stage the body image of the adolescent changes.

Erikson claims that the adolescent may feel uncomfortable about their body for a while until they can adapt and "grow into" the changes. Success in this stage will lead to the virtue of **fidelity**.

Fidelity involves being able to commit one's self to others on the basis of accepting others, even when there may be ideological differences.

During this period, they explore possibilities and begin to form their own identity based upon the outcome of their explorations. Failure to establish a sense of identity within society ("I don't know what I want to be when I grow up") can lead to role confusion. Role confusion involves the individual not being sure about themselves or their place in society.

In response to role confusion or **identity crisis**, an adolescent may begin to experiment with different lifestyles (e.g., work, education or political activities). Also pressuring someone into an identity can result in rebellion in the form of establishing a negative identity, and in addition to this feeling of unhappiness.

6. Intimacy vs. Isolation

Occurring in young adulthood (ages 18 to 40 yrs), we begin to share ourselves more intimately with others. We explore relationships leading toward longer-term commitments with someone other than a family member.

Successful completion of this stage can result in happy relationships and a sense of commitment, safety, and care within a relationship. Avoiding intimacy, fearing commitment and relationships can lead to isolation, loneliness, and sometimes depression. Success in this stage will lead to the virtue of **love**.

7. Generativity vs. Stagnation

During middle adulthood (ages 40 to 65 yrs), we establish our careers, settle down within a relationship, begin our own families and develop a sense of being a part of the bigger picture.

We give back to society through raising our children, being productive at work, and becoming involved in community activities and organizations.

By failing to achieve these objectives, we become stagnant and feel unproductive. Success in this stage will lead to the virtue of **care**.

8. Ego Integrity vs. Despair

As we grow older (65+ yrs) and become senior citizens, we tend to slow down our productivity and explore life as a retired person. It is during this time that we contemplate our accomplishments and can develop integrity if we see ourselves as leading a successful life.

Erik Erikson believed if we see our lives as unproductive, feel guilt about our past, or feel that we did not accomplish our life goals, we become dissatisfied with life and develop despair, often leading to depression and hopelessness.

Success in this stage will lead to the virtue of **wisdom**. Wisdom enables a person to look back on their life with a sense of closure and completeness, and also accept death without fear. Older people often enjoy sharing their wisdom.

CHAPTER 33

The Happiest Places On Earth

THE RESULTS ARE IN. HERE are this years happiest countries. It appears as though there is a pattern. But all is not what it seems to be. Many of the countries are cold many are Scandinavian. Denmark is almost always in the top two or three. In the next chapter, we will explain why.

Here they are, the happiest places on earth:

1. Norway
2. Denmark
3. Iceland
4. Switzerland
5. Finland
6. Netherlands
7. Canada
8. New Zealand
9. Australia
10. Sweden

CHAPTER 34

Orange Juice In Demark

—

DENMARK IS OFTEN NUMBER ONE or two in happiness research. Danes are just flat out happy people. A lot of hi ho hi ho going on in this small country just north of Germany and south of all of the Scandinavian countries,

The author traveled to Denmark to interview a lot of people and observe. Preliminary theories suggested that Danes did not have to worry about medical expenses, higher educational expenses, daycare, or housing, as the government makes sure these needs are met without people going into debt. The author's original theory also took into account a myriad of public services, such as public transportation, but this did not seem to be the answer to the question "Why are Danes so happy?"

The author interviewed many people in Tivoli Gardens, a beautiful little park in Copenhagen. This was actually the first place Walt Disney called the "happiest place on earth" and where he was inspired to build what we now call Disney Land and Disney World.

The folks walking about Tivoli Gardens were, to a person, happy. Happy to be there. As beautiful as it was, my native Chicago has larger more beautiful places in and around the city that dwarf Tivoli Garden.

The folks that were there were not thinking of other places they could go that might be nicer or larger, they were happy to be there. They were focused on being there.

I asked an older Danish man why Danes were so happy. He told me it was because they appreciated what they had; they were not thinking that there must be something better when they were involved in an experience. But he said he was worried. So I asked him why. He said he was worried because of Orange Juice. Orange juice? He explained that when he was young Orange Juice was in short supply and only available "in season" a brief time each year. Oh, how the people back then loved their Orange Juice!! It was a rare treat people savored, shared, and talked about. Now, it is available everyday, all year round.

People have it everyday. Now they take it for granted, and do not enjoy it much. He said he hoped there would not be many more Orange Juices.

There is a lesson to be learned here.

CHAPTER 35

Science Suggests Ten Ways To Become Happy

—

WE ALL WANT TO BE more productive, we want to accomplish more. One way to do that is to be happy. What does science tell us about this?

Here are 10 science-based ways to be happier from Belle Beth Cooper:

1. EXERCISE: 7 MINUTES COULD BE ENOUGH:

Seven minutes a day may be enough. (If you have time for more go for it!)

Exercise has such a profound effect on our happiness and well-being that it is an effective strategy for overcoming depression. In a study cited in Shawn Achor's book *The Happiness Advantage*; three groups of patients treated their depression with medication, exercise, or a combination of the two. The results of this study are informative: Although all three groups experienced similar improvements in their happiness levels early on, the follow-up assessments proved to be very different:

> *The groups were then tested six months later to assess their relapse rate. Of those who had taken the medication alone, 38 percent had slipped back into depression. Those in the combination group were doing only slightly better, with a 31 percent relapse rate. The biggest surprise, though, came from the exercise group: Their relapse rate was only 9 percent.*

You don't have to be depressed to benefit from exercise. Exercise can help you relax, increase your brainpower, and even improve your body image, even if you don't lose any weight.

Exercise has beneficial effects on our brains, such as releasing proteins and endorphins that make us feel happier.

A study in the *Journal of Health Psychology* found that people who exercised felt better about their bodies even when they saw no actual physical changes:

Body weight, shape and body image were assessed in 16 males and 18 females before and after both 6 × 40 minutes exercising and 6 × 40 minutes reading. Over both conditions, body weight and shape did not change. Various aspects of body image, however, improved after exercise compared to before.

Even if your actual appearance doesn't change, how you *feel* about your body does change.

2. Sleep More: You'll Be Less Sensitive to Negative Emotions

We know that sleep helps our body recover from the day and repair itself and that it helps us focus and be more productive. It turns out sleep is also very important for happiness.

In *NutureShock*, Po Bronson and Ashley Merryman explain how sleep affects positivity:

Negative stimuli get processed by the amygdala; positive or neutral memories gets processed by the hippocampus. Sleep deprivation hits the hippocampus harder than the amygdala. The result is that sleep-deprived people fail to recall pleasant memories yet recall gloomy memories just fine.

In one experiment by Walker, sleep-deprived college students tried to memorize a list of words. They could remember 81% of the words with a negative connotation, like "cancer." But they could remember only 31% of the words with a positive or neutral connotation, like "sunshine" or "basket."

The BPS Research Digest explores another study that proves sleep affects our sensitivity to negative emotions. Using a facial recognition task throughout the course of a day, researchers studied how sensitive participants were to positive and negative emotions. Those who worked through the afternoon without taking a nap became more sensitive to negative emotions like fear and anger.

Using a face recognition task, here we demonstrate an amplified reactivity to anger and fear emotions across the day, without sleep. However, an intervening nap blocked and even reversed this negative emotional reactivity to anger and fear while conversely enhancing ratings of positive (happy) expressions.

Of course, how well (and how long) you sleep will probably affect how you feel when you wake up, which can make a difference to your whole day.

Another study tested how employees' moods when they started work in the morning affected their entire workday.

Researchers found that employees' moods when they clocked in tended to affect how they felt the rest of the day. Early mood was linked to their perceptions of customers and to how they reacted to customers' moods.

And most importantly to managers, employee mood had a clear impact on performance, including both how much work employees did and how well they did it.

3. Spend More Time With Friends/Family: Money Can't Buy You Happiness

Staying in touch with friends and family is one of the top five regrets of the dying.

If you want more evidence that time with friends is beneficial for you, research proves it can make you happier right now, too.

Social time is highly valuable when it comes to improving our happiness, even for introverts. Several studies have found that time spent with friends and family makes a big difference to how happy we feel.

Harvard explains it:

We are happy when we have family, we are happy when we have friends and almost all the other things we think make us happy are actually just ways of getting more family and friends.

George Vaillant is the director of a 72-year study of the lives of 268 men.

In an interview in the March 2008 newsletter to the Grant Study subjects, Vaillant was asked, "What have you learned from the Grant Study men?" Vaillant's response: "That the only thing that really matters in life are your relationships to other people."

He shared insights of the study with Joshua Wolf Shenk at *The Atlantic* on how men's social connections made a difference to their overall happiness:

Men's relationships at age 47, he found, predicted late-life adjustment better than any other variable. Good sibling relationships seem especially powerful: 93 percent of the men who were thriving at age 65 had been close to a brother or sister when younger.

In fact, a study published in the *Journal of Socio-Economics* states than your relationships are worth more than $100,000:

Using the British Household Panel Survey, I find that an increase in the level of social involvements is worth up to an extra £85,000 a year in terms of life satisfaction. Actual changes in income, on the other hand, buy very little happiness.

I think that last line is especially fascinating: *Actual changes in income, on the other hand, buy very little happiness.* So we could increase our annual income by hundreds of thousands of dollars and still not be as happy as we would if we increased the strength of our social relationships.

The Terman study, covered in *The Longevity Project*, found that relationships and how we help others were important factors in living long, happy lives:

> *We figured that if a Terman participant sincerely felt that he or she had friends and relatives to count on when having a hard time then that person would be healthier. Those who felt very loved and cared for, we predicted, would live the longest.*

> *Surprise: our prediction was wrong... Beyond social network size, the clearest benefit of social relationships came from helping others. Those who helped their friends and neighbors, advising and caring for others, tended to live to old age.*

4. GET OUTSIDE MORE: HAPPINESS IS MAXIMIZED AT 57°

In *The Happiness Advantage*, Shawn Achor recommends spending time in the fresh air to improve your happiness:

> *Making time to go outside on a nice day also delivers a huge advantage; one study found that spending 20 minutes outside in good weather not only boosted positive mood, but also broadened thinking and improved working memory...*

This is pretty good news for those of us who are worried about fitting new habits into our already-busy schedules. Twenty minutes is a short enough time to spend outside that you could fit it into your commute or even your lunch break.

A UK study from the University of Sussex also found that being outdoors made people happier:

> *Being outdoors, near the sea, on a warm, sunny weekend afternoon is the perfect spot for most. In fact, participants were found to be substantially happier outdoors in all natural environments than they were in urban environments.*

The American Meteorological Society published research in 2011 that found current temperature has a bigger effect on our happiness than variables like wind speed and humidity, or even the average temperature over the course of a day. It also found that happiness is maximized at 57 degrees (13.9°C), so keep an eye on the weather forecast before heading outside for your 20 minutes of fresh air.

The connection between productivity and temperature is another topic we've talked about more here. It's fascinating what a small change in temperature can do.

5. Help Others: 100 Hours a Year is the Magic Number

One of the most counterintuitive pieces of advice I found is that to make yourself feel happier, you should help others. In fact, 100 hours per year (or two hours per week) is the optimal time we should dedicate to helping others in order to enrich our lives.

If we go back to Shawn Achor's book again, he says this about helping others:

> *...When researchers interviewed more than 150 people about their recent purchases, they found that money spent on activities--such as concerts and group dinners out--brought far more pleasure than material purchases like shoes, televisions, or expensive watches. Spending money on other people, called "prosocial spending," also boosts happiness.*

The Journal of Happiness Studies published a study that explored this very topic:

> *Participants recalled a previous purchase made for either himself or herself or someone else and then reported their happiness. Afterward, participants chose whether to spend a monetary windfall on himself or herself or*

someone else. Participants assigned to recall a purchase made for someone else reported feeling significantly happier immediately after this recollection; most importantly, the happier participants felt, the more likely they were to choose to spend a windfall on someone else in the near future.

So spending money on other people makes us happier than buying stuff for ourselves. But what about spending our *time* on other people?

A study of volunteering in Germany explored how volunteers were affected when their opportunities to help others were taken away:

Shortly after the fall of the Berlin Wall but before the German reunion, the first wave of data of the GSOEP was collected in East Germany. Volunteering was still widespread. Due to the shock of the reunion, a large portion of the infrastructure of volunteering (e.g. sports clubs associated with firms) collapsed and people randomly lost their opportunities for volunteering. Based on a comparison of the change in subjective well-being of these people and of people from the control group who had no change in their volunteer status, the hypothesis is supported that volunteering is rewarding in terms of higher life satisfaction.

In his book *Flourish: A Visionary New Understanding of Happiness and Well-being*, University of Pennsylvania professor Martin Seligman explains that helping others can improve our own lives:

...We scientists have found that doing a kindness produces the single most reliable momentary increase in well-being of any exercise we have tested.

6. Practice Smiling: Reduce Pain, Improve Mood, Think Better

Smiling can make us feel better, but it's more effective when we back it up with positive thoughts, according to this study:

A new study led by a Michigan State University business scholar suggests customer-service workers who fake smile throughout the day worsen their mood and withdraw from work, affecting productivity. But workers who smile as a result of cultivating positive thoughts--such as a tropical vacation or a child's recital--improve their mood and withdraw less.

Of course it's important to practice "real smiles" where you use your eye sockets. (You've seen fake smiles that don't reach the person's eyes. Try it. Smile with just your mouth. Then smile naturally; your eyes narrow. There's a huge difference in a fake smile and a genuine smile.)

According to PsyBlog, smiling can improve our attention and help us perform better on cognitive tasks:

Smiling makes us feel good which also increases our attentional flexibility and our ability to think holistically. When this idea was tested by Johnson et al. (2010), the results showed that participants who smiled performed better on attentional tasks which required seeing the whole forest rather than just the trees.

A smile is also a good way to reduce some of the pain we feel in troubling circumstances:

Smiling is one way to reduce the distress caused by an upsetting situation. Psychologists call this the facial feedback hypothesis. Even forcing a smile when we don't feel like it is enough to lift our mood slightly (this is one example of embodied cognition).

7. Plan a Trip: It Helps Even if You Don't Actually Take One

As opposed to actually taking a holiday, simply *planning* a vacation or break from work can improve our happiness. A study published in the journal

Applied Research in Quality of Lifeshowed that the highest spike in happiness came during the planning stage of a vacation as people enjoy the sense of anticipation:

In the study, the effect of vacation anticipation boosted happiness for eight weeks. After the vacation, happiness quickly dropped back to baseline levels for most people.

Shawn Achor has some info for us on this point, as well:

One study found that people who just thought about watching their favorite movie actually raised their endorphin levels by 27 percent.

If you can't take the time for a vacation right now, or even a night out with friends, put something on the calendar--even if it's a month or a year down the road. Then, whenever you need a boost of happiness, remind yourself about it.

8. MEDITATE: REWIRE YOUR BRAIN FOR HAPPINESS

Meditation is often touted as an important habit for improving focus, clarity, and attention span, as well as helping to keep you calm. It turns out it's also useful for improving your happiness:

In one study, a research team from Massachusetts General Hospital looked at the brain scans of 16 people before and after they participated in an eight-week course in mindfulness meditation. The study, published in the January issue of Psychiatry Research: Neuroimaging, concluded that after completing the course, parts of the participants' brains associated with compassion and self-awareness grew, and parts associated with stress shrank.

Meditation literally clears your mind and calms you down; it's been often proven to be the single most effective way to live a happier life. According to Achor, meditation can actually make you happier long-term:

Studies show that in the minutes right after meditating, we experience feelings of calm and contentment, as well as heightened awareness and empathy. And, research even shows that regular meditation can permanently rewire the brain to raise levels of happiness.

The fact that we can actually alter our brain structure through mediation is most surprising to me and somewhat reassuring that however we feel and think today isn't permanent.

9. Move Closer to Work: A Short Commute is Worth More Than a Big House

Our commute to work can have a surprisingly powerful impact on our happiness. The fact that we tend to commute twice a day at least five days a week makes it unsurprising that the effect would build up over time and make us less and less happy.

According to *The Art of Manliness*, having a long commute is something we often fail to realize will affect us so dramatically:

… while many voluntary conditions don't affect our happiness in the long term because we acclimate to them, people never get accustomed to their daily slog to work because sometimes the traffic is awful and sometimes it's not.

Or as Harvard psychologist Daniel Gilbert put it, "Driving in traffic is a different kind of hell every day."

We tend to try to compensate for this by having a bigger house or a better job, but these compensations just don't work:

Two Swiss economists who studied the effect of commuting on happiness found that such factors could not make up for the misery created by a long commute.

10. Practice Gratitude: Increase Happiness and Satisfaction

This is a seemingly simple strategy but I've personally found it to make a huge difference to my outlook. There are lots of ways to practice gratitude, from keeping a journal of things you're grateful for, sharing three good things that happen each day with a friend or your partner, and going out of your way to show gratitude when others help you.

In an experiment where participants took note of things they were grateful for each day, their moods were improved just from this simple practice:

The gratitude-outlook groups exhibited heightened well-being across several, though not all, of the outcome measures across the three studies, relative to the comparison groups. The effect on positive affect appeared to be the most robust finding. Results suggest that a conscious focus on blessings may have emotional and interpersonal benefits.

The Journal of Happiness studies published a study that used letters of gratitude to test how being grateful can affect our levels of happiness:

Participants included 219 men and women who wrote three letters of gratitude over a 3-week period. Results indicated that writing letters of gratitude increased participants' happiness and life satisfaction while decreasing depressive symptoms.

Quick Final Fact: Getting Older Will Actually Make You Happier As we get older, particularly past middle age, we tend to naturally grow happier. There's still some debate over why this happens, but scientists have a few ideas:

Researchers, including the authors, have found that older people shown pictures of faces or situations tend to focus on and remember the happier ones more and the negative ones less.

Other studies have discovered that as people age, they seek out situations that will lift their moods--for instance, pruning social circles of friends or acquaintances who might bring them down. Still other work finds that older adults learn to let go of loss and disappointment over unachieved goals, and focus their goals on greater well-being.

So if you thought getting old would make you miserable, it's likely you'll develop a more positive outlook than you probably have now.

How cool is that?

CHAPTER 36

Gross National Happiness

—

CAN MONEY MAKE YOU HAPPY? Prime Minister Tschering Tobgay of Bhutan suggests that it may not.

Research suggests that after we have achieved a basic living standard (which varies from nation to nation) more money does **not** lead to proportionally greater happiness. In 2018 the nation of Bhutan will apply its efforts to this issue.

For more than sixty years Bhutan has developed its society in accordance with the philosophy of Gross National Happiness (GNH). Many nations are keen to utilize this concept, especially in the realm of business. Several countries are beginning to see the value of getting companies to pursue long-term policies that sustain a responsible business as opposed to short-term policies that emphasize quick profits.

GNH promotes a societies happiness via a balanced, inclusive, sustainable, and **equitable** model of development. In Bhutan, the government is attempting to get business to buy into the concept of GDH. Businesses are encouraged to be accountable to their employees, shareholders, customers, their communities, and the environment.

Bhutan is starting a GNH certification process for businesses developed from the GNH Index that has shaped the public policy of Bhutan. This process involves indicators in nine domains of societies GNH that cover the impact on workers, consumers, the community as well as the business itself. The information on four of the domains: psychological well-being, health, time use, and education, will be collected from a companies employees. For the other five domains: community vitality, cultural diversity, good governance, ecological diversity, and living standards, data will be sourced from the company.

Gross National Happiness (also known by the acronym: **GNH**) is a developing philosophy as well as an "index" which is used to measure the collective happiness in any specific nation.

The concept was first mentioned in the Constitution of Bhutan, which was enacted on 18 July 2008.

The term "gross national happiness" was coined by the fourth king of Bhutan, Jigme Singye Wangchuck, in the 1970s.

The GNH's central tenets are: "sustainable and equitable socio-economic development; environmental conservation; preservation and promotion of culture; and good governance"

GNH is distinguishable b, for example, valuing collective happiness as the goal of governance, and by emphasizing harmony with nature and traditional values.

The implementation of a GNH policy can be challenging, as it requires considerable institutional support. In Bhutan, the implementation – or mainstreaming – of GNH into political institutions has been a gradual process for several decades but recently accelerated with the introduction of the GNH Index and the GNH Screening Tool.

As part of a lengthy and ongoing process of integrating the GNH philosophy into public policy, the GNH Index was developed by the <u>Centre for Bhutan Studies</u> (CBS) to help measure the progress of Bhutanese society. In 2010, the first nationwide GNH survey was conducted with a sample size of 8,510 Bhutanese aged 15 and above. The second nationwide survey was conducted in 2015 and had a sample size of 8,871. After all three rounds of surveys, follow-up interviews and additional data gathering was conducted in order to review and refine the survey. The GNH survey covers all twenty districts (Dzonkhag) and results are reported for varying demographic factors such as gender, age, abode, and occupation. The survey therefore provides a rich dataset to compare the happiness between different groups of citizens, and how this has changed over time.

In Bhutan, the government has taken an active role in developing a society built on the concept that happiness involves more than money.

While the author agrees with the concept of GNH, Sophie Tucker, in the interest of fairness, must be given equal time:

"I've been rich and I've been poor. Rich is better."

— Sophie Tucker

CHAPTER 37

Get Your Dam Dog

—

EVERY SO OFTEN THE AUTHOR and the person he is related to by marriage go to Las Vegas to see the wonderful shows and the Hoover Dam. The Hoover Dam is so impressive one never gets tired of touring it. For the record, there is no gambling on these trips.

One year they sold a Dam Dog after you toured the inside of this amazing structure. The Dam Dog was 18 inches of impressive encased meats that came with a hard hat, a t-shirt, and indigestion. The author's better half suggested I get the dam dog, something that I certainly would have enjoyed. When you are from Chicago, Hot Dogs are important, and an 18-inch sausage would not prove to be a challenge. I declined saying that I would get it next time.

For three years I thought about this Dam Dog and the Dam Dog was the primary motivation for the next trip.

The next time we went, there was the Dam but no Dam Dog.

The lesson is: GET YOUR DAM DOG.

CHAPTER 38

Top Ten Happy Songs

---

1. Happy Together. - The Turtles (How can anything by a group called The Turtles not make you happy? By the way, are you a turtle?)
2. Don't Worry, Be Happy. —Bobby Mc Farrin (You won't feel bad about forgetting the rent check.)
3. The Happy Organ. "Baby" Cortez
4. My Happiness-Connie Francis
5. If You Wanna Be Happy-Jimmy Soul
6. You've Made Me So Very Happy-Blood, Sweat, and Tears
7. Love Can Make You Happy. -Mercy
8. Happy Days. -Pratt and McClain
9. Happy Birthday Sweet Sixteen. -Neil Sedaka
10. Sha-La-La.-The Reverend Al Green

Top Ten Happy Movies

---

1. Big Fish
2. Remember The Titans
3. Little Miss Sunshine
4. Ground Hog Day
5. Slumdog Millionaire
6. Down With Love
7. Pursuit of Happyness
8. Billy Elliot
9. Precious
10. Stepmom

Top Ten Happy Books

—

10% Happier by Dan Harris

Synposis: Meditation can help you focus on the present moment rather than worry about the future. Improve your health, sharpen your focus and enjoy a sense of inner calm. Start by sitting quietly for five minutes and just focus on your breathing.

The Art of Happiness by the Dalai Lama

Synopsis: When life gets complicated, take a step back and remind yourself of your overall purpose or goal. Reflect on what will truly bring you happiness and then reset your priorities accordingly; this can give you a fresh perspective on what direction to take.

Authentic Happiness by Martin E.P. Seligman

Synopsis: What is the good life? It's actually a simple path. A pleasant life might be champagne and a sports car, but the good life is using your signature strengths every day to produce authentic happiness and abundant gratification. Written by the founder of the positive psychology movement.

The Four Agreements by Don Miguel Ruiz

Synopsis: 1. Be impeccable with your word and speak with integrity. 2. Don't take anything personally and realize people say and do things because of their own reality. 3. Don't make assumptions and communicate clearly with others. 4. Always do your best. There, now you don't even have to read the book.

The Happiness Advantage by Shawn Achor

Synopsis: Insights gained from Harvard studies on happiness include: Habits are like financial capital. Forming one today is an investment that will automatically give out returns for years to come.

The Happiness Project by Gretchen Rubin

Synopsis: Are you focused on the things that really matter to you? Set measurable goals in an area of your life you want to improve (marriage, parenting, work, self-fulfillment) and build on those goals cumulatively with specific action steps. For example, increase your energy by going to bed early, getting organized and exercising more.

The Gifts of Imperfection by Brene Brown

Synopsis: Give up perfection. Take risks and put your true self out into the world. Use courage, compassion and connection to live a fuller life. Each day think, "I am enough."

The Magic of Thinking Big by David J. Schwartz

Synopsis: Believe it can be done and you will succeed. When you really believe, your mind will find the ways to do it. Believing in a solution paves the way to making that solution a reality.

The Slight Edge by Jeff Olson

Synopsis: It's great to have dreams and aspirations, says Live Happy founder Jeff Olson. But it's the small things we do in the moment that have a cumulative, compounding effect. You can achieve anything you want, but the only way to make it happen is not through quantum leaps, but by doing the little things over and over every single day.

Stumbling on Happiness by Daniel Gilbert

Synopsis: We aren't very good at predicting what will make us happy, says Harvard professor Gilbert. Challenge what your imagination dreams up for the future. Strike a balance between feeling good enough to cope with a situation but bad enough to do something about it. Use your emotions as a compass to tell you what to do.